Through My Lens Poetry

Mission: To Proclaim Transformation and Truth

Publisher: Transformed Publishing, Cocoa, FL

Website: www.transformedpublishing.com

Email: transformedpublishing@gmail.com

ISBN: 978-1-953241-43-6

Through
My Lens
Poetry

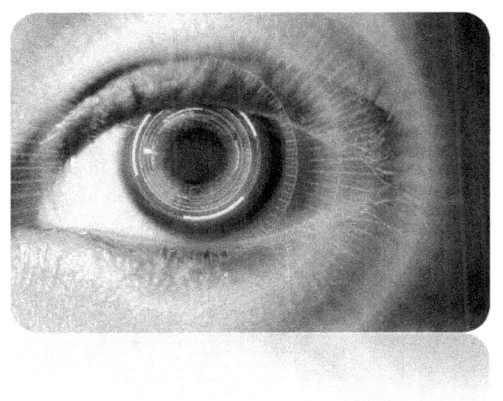

Derisha
Blocker

Preface

On June 8th 2022, I heard the Lord say "Get into position!" After I heard that, the Scripture Jeremiah 29:11 came to mind. I quickly grabbed my Bible and flipped it open, and it read:

> For I know the thoughts that I think toward you, says the Lord, thoughts of peace and not of evil, to give you a future and a hope.
> -Jeremiah 29:11

During this time, I was contemplating writing poems. I had some written already but wasn't sure I should keep writing. I also had titles written down for a book. With this Scripture and God's words, I continued to move forward and intentionally started writing poems. Although it wasn't easy, and most days I was exhausted, I was still able to move and get into position.

Dedication

To young people and adults who have given up, fought depression and anxiety, or questioned their purpose, you are not alone. May this encourage you to keep going knowing that God got you every step of the way.

To my grandmas, Marion Blocker and Barbara Bush, thank you for encouraging me and telling me that I'm doing a great job in life even when sometimes I feel differently. Your words of wisdom are appreciated and I'm so glad to have you both as my grandmothers.

To my grandfathers, Lonnie Blocker and Dennis Moss who have went on to glory, I miss you both so much. You both loved me so much and I knew that. Thank you, grandad Blocker, for telling me not to give up in your last months. Grandad Dennis thank you for laughter and motivation. I know you both would be super proud of me. I carry you both in my heart.

To my mother, thank you for telling me to keep striving for excellence no matter what. Your love for me is great and I appreciate everything you do for me. Through my tears and fears you have been the one to really help me back up. Reassuring me that God indeed has a plan for my life, even when I don't understand it. I love you so much.

Table of Contents

Introduction 1

Pain & Prize 2

HOPE 3

Still Here in a Different Light 4

Frustrated 5

Black Excellence 6

Black History 7

We are History 8

Women's History 9

WATER 10

Every Day 11

Help 12

Light Every Time 13

I AM 14

Standing 15

Journey 16

Choice 17

UP and UP 18

Greatness 19

Valuable 20

Peace 21

Ever Wonder? 22

Don't Quit 23

One Day 24

Bad Days 25

Psalm 23   26
Light   27
Overcoming Hate   28
In the Mirror   30
Learning   32
Win & Lose   33
Myself   34
AIR   35
Don't Stop   36
MOSS   37
I AM ME   38
All the Time   39
L.B.   40
Good Place   41
Changing Me For _Me_   42
Not Alone   43
Life Over Death   44
Sonshine   45
I Learned   46
Focused   48
Sigh   49
Epilogue   50
Final Message   51
About the Author   53

Introduction

The first section of poems in this collection reignited my fire to write again. Originally, they were written to celebrate black history month. As I wrote, I remembered being a little girl, writing poems every night, about how I was feeling and other things and events that happened in my life. I would share these poems with my mother and stepfather. They always complimented how good they were.

As I got older, the fire was put out and I stopped writing entirely. I am glad my fire is ablaze and that I am writing again. I pray that you enjoy these poems and can maybe even relate to some of them in a way that can help you reflect and evaluate yourself by looking into some of my experiences emotionally and mentally. I am still standing only by God's mercy and grace. Remember that forgiving, healing, and moving from past hurts, is a long continuous process. It cannot be done in microwave time.

Derisha
Blocker

Pain & Prize

For what it's worth
Pain comes with a prize
Tears fall because of tares
Brokenness hurts
In the end
We've cried
We've shouted
We've sat down
Only to get back up
Left foot, then right
We stand tall in the middle of the fight
Legs weakened
Eyes burning
Many before us endured
How on God's green earth
Are we still here?
Many hate us
Many don't believe us
Proven by our lineage
Pain comes with a prize.

HOPE

We've encountered A-LOT
To get where we are today
We've climbed mountains
Walked for hours
We've sung, songs
We've prayed, prayers
We've used peaceful tactics
But yet
That seems like it wasn't enough
We keep on holding on
Holding on for our children
And our children for their children
We stay steadfast
And hold tight
Onto hope
For change
For new beginnings.

Derisha
Blocker

Still Here in a Different Light

Just like a child's first words

Mama and Dada

The world brings first time things like
viruses, diseases, businesses, and careers

For us

What we watched and what we experience is not the first

It is not brand new

A whole lot of centuries ago it started

All because one man looked different than the other

Our response then had to be, "Yes sir, yes masta,"

To prevent bodily harm

Held hostage

We had to do what was necessary

We had to obey

To protect our loved ones and ourselves

After all the time that has passed

Our obedience and proof of humanity still would not suffice

Now in the 21st century
we still have what I heard my grandma talk about

Many say we have come a long way

Be we have a mighty long way to go.

Frustrated!

Who do you think I am?

A black girl who can't see or figure out every
clue you've given by just talking through your lips.

You have no intentions to fulfill what you're saying.

I am a leader and it comes naturally so it's in me.

I've led and have done everything that was
asked but yet I am told no one ever gets a 9 or a 10.

I might not have gotten in that range according to you.

But through my lens, my talents
are worth more than a score of a 6.

We all have space to grow and
learn even if we reach a score of a 10.

You never stop improving and you
certainly don't stop bettering yourself in life.

My choice about my availability being
limited is so people like you won't take advantage.

Advantage of a hard-working
dedicated melanin woman like me.

I refuse to allow you or anybody
else to use me without proper numbers.

Titles are earned and should never just be given.

But when someone like me has a darker
pigmentation, we are used, overlooked, & pressured.

Not given what we deserve
because of your bias or discrimination.

Derisha
Blocker

Black Excellence

Kings and queens
Majestic and royalty purple and gold
High class
Walk with shoulders back
Head high and eyes forward
Showing boldness and assurance
There is a quickness to the responses
But slow enough to hear every comment
Dark and as beautiful as the night sky
This is
For everyone with the skin tone
Copper or darker
Shine and shine bright

Black History

We say black is beautiful

Black is strong

Black is intelligent

Black is history

We have road maps, books, magazines, and documentaries

Today, right now

Can our black men be beautiful, strong, intelligent, and history

Can our black women be beautiful, strong, intelligent, and history

It is time to hold us accountable

To continue to raise our children according to our legacy

Our history

It's time to make a difference again.

Derisha
Blocker

We are History

We are history
It runs through our blood down in our veins
It's our thick, wooly, soft, and big fro
Our natural hair that shows our growth
It shows our beauty
To be natural and real
Our skin melting like chocolate
Shining like freshly shined bronze
Standing out so beautifully
So much melanin
That we stand out in the biggest crowds
Our brains of intelligence and knowledge
Ideas and creativeness
Shows our history
We know how to stand in the gap and fight
for what is right
We are history.

Women's History

When it's *Women's History Month* stop and say,

Well done!

Well done in labor

Well done as a single parent

Well done!

For being strong even when all odds were stacked against you

Well done!

For powering up on days when you were so low

Well done!

For being a woman and keeping one foot in front of the other

Well done!

In making a difference in your family and in your community

Well done!

For making history that will be known forever.

Derisha
Blocker

W
A
T
E
R

Like full buckets of water

Like an ocean

Like a pool full of chlorine water

Like rain puddles after a storm

Like a waterfall in front of an office

Like the droplets in a rainforest

Like a wet mop dripping water

My soul is full - full of overflowing water

It runs from my eyes, falling slowly down each cheek

It runs to my mouth and then drips from my chin down to my feet

It is so much so that I have lost count

It is a miracle I am still here and not drowned in all this water

It is a miracle to be writing this

It is a miracle to survive this tsunami of tears.

Every Day

waking up motionless no energy, no energy
just my spirit in my body and my body standing in a room on earth
see I have tried so many things to be great to be a success
trying was not good enough because I still failed the test
day in and day out I would encourage others, that is who I am
they were suffering
they were struggling
they were hurting
they were crying
I stopped for a moment; I realized that in my own life I was struggling
many times, I threw in the towel, sat down, and totally gave up
every day it seemed like it was a tropical storm
I thought, "I'm not getting anywhere!"
I cried out, "GOD!"
but my cry was not answered
so, like before I sat down, trying to pull hope from everywhere
but it could not be found
I refocused after I hung my head and threw in the towel for a while
I was down but decided to get up
one day this cycle will be broken and motionless will become motion
motion is here and I'm learning to help myself every day.

Derisha
Blocker

11

Help

Doubt and frustration
Nowhere to turn, no friends no family
No one to turn to
Even God seems far away,
what to do when you feel like you're losing
You're the only one in this realm,
the only one who knows the strength of the winds
Yet deep down you know,
you're not the only one that's been here
Who has encountered this once or twice in a lifetime
You feel like you're drowning,
better yet like you're suffocating
Trying hard to catch your breath,
so that you can utter HIS name Jesus
Help, your daughter of Zion is suffering,
only to find out
That longsuffering was part of His plan for you
To make you stronger, better, and greater
The Lord will see you through this phase of your life
While building strong endurance
Look to Him for guidance.

Scripture Reading: Romans 5:3-5 (ESV)
[M]ore than that, we rejoice in our sufferings,
knowing that suffering produces endurance,
and endurance produces character, and
character produces hope, and hope does not
put us to shame, because God's love has been
poured into our hearts through the Holy Spirit
who has been given to us.

Through
My Lens
Poetry

Light Every Time

Swallowed up in your tears

Swallowed up in your fears

Swallowed up in darkness

No light

But just like darkness tries to close you up

Light comes, to burst you out

Light brings joy in place of tears

It brings peace in place of fears

Light is stronger, so next time darkness comes

Remind yourself that you are light

And light overtakes darkness every time.

I AM

I am who I say I am

Not who you say I am

I am a conqueror

I am a champion

In the end I have the victory

I am who I say I am.

Through
My Lens
Poetry

standing

Stand tall, stand upright

Head up, shoulders back

Tears falling but you're still standing

Stand tall, stand upright

Not looking back

Just remembering where you came from

Stand tall, stand upright

Keep walking, keep fighting

No one by your side

Stand tall, stand upright

Success can be a lonely road, many before you made it

They had fire on every side,

You have fire, but you are such a different light

Stand tall, stand upright

You can stay steadfast, you will keep going

You are standing.

Derisha
Blocker

Journey

His plans for me are good, I know this to be true
However, when the tears drop, not tears of happiness,
joy, gladness, gratefulness, or accomplishments
But tears of what is next, I don't know what to do
Has He forgotten about me, does He hear me
The questions of *why?*
The constant questions of *what is next?*

Choice

Peace is mine

Love is mine

Joy is mine

Laughter and smiles

Are all mine.

Derisha
Blocker

UP

and

UP

Look up, hold your head up
When it feels like the world is on your shoulders
Take a deep breath
Know that it can only get better from here
You fall, then get back up
You stumble
Then reposition your posture
Look up, hold your head up
Up is your destination
Up is where you're going
Up is your place
Keep looking up.

Greatness

Does the way I walk intimidate you?
The way I talk make you uncomfortable?
The way I move make you annoyed?
Is there a problem?

I'm content and very happy with who I am
I hope you find peace and joy to be
Your authentic self
I'm already living and being me
I am a woman of power
A woman of grace
A woman of boldness and strength
I talk with strength
I take steps in boldness
I am a weapon created to destroy negativity
So, I hope and pray that you find your
greatness because where I tread
There is greatness
If you need help do not get offended
Ask so I can pull you along
On this greatness train.

Derisha
Blocker

19

Valuable

I am worth it
I am worth the wait
I am worth the time and energy
That someone put towards for my benefit
I am worth more than gold
I am worth more than silver
I am valuable
And I will make sure everyone who I deal with
Knows my worth
No more settling
No more sugar coating
No more being nice
I am worth it, because of this
Change is my portion
Newness is my portion
I am changed forever.

Peace

The wind underneath our feet

The breeze touching our face

The sunlight glistening on our sugar-coated skin

The silence of nature

But the loudness of the silence, was everything

The stillness of time

When we sat just to be sitting

Oh, how that was a moment, I will treasure forever

And ever.

Derisha
Blocker

Ever Wonder?

I wonder, do you wonder?

What life would be like if you were born in another century

If you could gain wings like an eagle and soar in the spacious sky

If there were visiting hours in eternity

Do you wonder?

What it would be like to escape to a place

Where only the serenity stands and captivates your entire being

Ever wonder?

What life would be like

Living in a wonder

And existing, wonderfully.

Don't Quit

Fall but get back up

Cry but dry your eyes

Be sick and tired but keep going

Be mad and afterwards forgive

Shake your head but know trouble don't last always

Hold your head down just for a second and know
looking up is better

Sit down over and over again

But get back up again and again

Feel faint

But don't grow weary in well doing

It's a *must* for the sake of your calling for the sake
of your destiny

Jump over bridges

Climb every mountain

Every door shut, another opens

Walk through, run through

Better is coming, to you, for you

   -Your life depends on you.

One Day

One day it will be my time to shine to stand up and declare the greatness

Of every woman, to speak truth

Standing boldly as the woman I was created to be

Silence won't have a place on the inside of me and fear won't control me

I will speak, I will walk, I will be the great woman the earth needs

One day, and that day starts now!

Bad Days

Days in life can be so uncertain

It can be so alone, so dim, so scary

Life was given with a purpose and a plan to fulfill that purpose

However, the plan does not come with clear instructions

Instead, you get hit with surprises & mysteries along the way

For me I have been walking this journey alone in the dark & scared

I've cried, carried anger, and I try my best not to give up

I've walked around with frowns,
with blank stares, and even with my head hung down

Yet here I am writing and expressing days in life

Concerning my walk

If you can relate just know you're not alone

I've been there

Just like others who came out on the winning side

We are next

We are coming out of days in life

Of uncertainty, fear, anger, and loneliness

Better days are ahead

Because of a few bad days here and there,
let's not let it knock us down

And we not fight to get back up
Get up and declare better days are coming.

Derisha
Blocker

Scripture Reading: PSALM 23

The Lord is my shepherd;

I shall not want.

He makes me to lie down in green pastures;

He leads me beside the still waters.

He restores my soul;

He leads me in the paths of righteousness

For His name's sake.

Yea, though I walk through the valley of the
shadow of death,

I will fear no evil;

For You are with me;

Your rod and Your staff, they comfort me.

You prepare a table before me in the presence
of my enemies;

You anoint my head with oil;

My cup runs over.

Surely goodness and mercy shall follow me

All the days of my life;

And I will dwell in the house of the Lord

FOREVER.

Through
My Lens
Poetry

Light!

Is it me or does anybody feel drained in these last few years

A lot is happening, yet a lot is not

A lot of noise, darkness, confusion

A lot of heartache, tears, fears, and a lot of questions

What is *not* happening

Where is the light?

Last time I checked light over powers darkness every time

Where is the light?

When will the light rise up

Rise up with purpose

Rise with a voice

Rise with hope

Rise to do what our Creator called us to do

Let's reverse draining to recovering, strengthening

And walking to change this year and the years to come.

Scripture Reading: Isaiah 60:1-3
Arise, shine;
For your light has come!
And the glory of the Lord is risen upon you.
For behold, the darkness shall cover the earth,
And deep darkness the people;
But the Lord will arise over you,
And His glory will be seen upon you.
The Gentiles shall come to your light,
And kings to the brightness of your rising.

Derisha
Blocker

Overcoming Hate

I would stop if no one was counting on me

I have been put aside by so many and shut out by many

That stopping would bring life to their bones

So many times, their negative comments have done damage

But I've taken that damage to keep moving forward

Many have turned their backs,
walked away, completely ignored me

I have given so much to them all

Not once have I called them out of their name

I am a true believer you reap what you sow

I work hard, and push by hateful people

It is the sly comments

The raise of the eyebrow

That make me keep going even though

Deep down an encouraging word would do good to my soul

I pray that our Creator touches your heart just like He has mine

I will keep going no matter what

I am overcoming hate.

When we encounter those who have hurt us, talked about us, and wronged us; it is important to forgive. We can be upset for a moment but always forgive. Remember it is a process so you might have to forgive them often until you free yourself from what they have done to you.

Scripture Reading: Ephesians 4:26-27 & 32
"Be angry, and do not sin": do not let the sun go down on your wrath, nor give place to the devil.

And be kind to one another, tenderhearted, forgiving one another, even as God in Christ forgave you.

In the Mirror

Take a moment and look in the mirror

The image looking back is not sure they like what they see

They have been told if you don't like what you see change it

If you don't like something in your life change it

They have done what they know to do

And things remain the same

What I realize between individuals in the mirror

And those who say, "Change it!"

They have super support great or small

They have someone or people - a support system

The super support wants to see them win

To reach every dream, every hope

Make every impossible thing possible

They have resources

They have the love of others to win

The one in the mirror

With little to no resources

No support system

No one *that* willing to endure to help

They like but do not love

What to do to win?

To change their story

They have pushed so hard

Have cried many times

Frustration has taken over for so many years

Trying to figure it out on their own

Those who are successful have endured hardship and difficulty

I don't understand why assumptions are made that every man

Or woman must take the same route

When they have answers to make the load a little lighter

What is it that says

I didn't have it easy

So, because you didn't have it easy

Can you not give what you went through or what you learned to others

So they can make it

Why not shine your light on someone else's darkness

This world is not getting any easier

If you can give something to someone who is struggling

Why not, why not

Help the one in the mirror to win, to succeed, to change their lives

Just as you did.

Derisha
Blocker

Learning

Just like a child learning ways of life
I too am learning, learning how to grow
To accept the stretching, the bending
The breaking to mature me

Just like faith a parent believes
Their child will grow and begin to understand
This same faith my Father in heaven has for me
In my doubt He believes I can

He believes and knows I will grow
That I will mature daily
This walk is one that can get weary along the way
However, I choose to continue

No matter what it takes
I will succeed, I will grow
I will win in the end.

Win & Lose

I win I win

    I lose I lose

        I take hits

            I take high fives

                I take the ups

            And I take the downs

        I win in the morning

    And can lose by day

But day by day

        I choose my outcome

        I win I win

            I lose I lose

        No matter what life throws

    If I lose I still

Choose opposite of my opposition

    No matter what comes

        No matter who goes

        I look up

            Up

            And UP.

Derisha
Blocker

33

Myself

I'm a woman
A woman who has seen a whole lot
Heard a whole lot
Watched a whole lot
And listened a whole lot

Live my life learning
Battling each day with strength from above
I had days that tripped me and knocked me out
Days of good and bad
Days where I witnessed good and evil

With all I have seen
All I have done
My life experiences have grown me up
Taught me to walk tall
Even when the weight of words
And the cuts from eyes
Pierced me and cause me to question myself

Through it all
All the ups and downs
I have chosen not to fold
To not be who others think I should be
I walk and continue to walk as me
Even when others don't understand me
And some don't like what they see

I choose me every time
I continue to grow, continue to learn
And continue to love myself
And encourage myself.

Through
My Lens
Poetry

AIR

Inhale the air
The air of goodness and greatness
The air of change and transformation
The air that we breathe gives life
The life that we have is not an accident
It is purposeful it is intentional
The air is so refreshing
The breeze that we feel
Allows the air that we breathe to bring peace
Take it all in and inhale the air
The air of newness
The air of change
Feel the rhythm of the air
Walk to the beat of its drum
Towards light electricity
Take a deep breath and know
That the air breathed, is the life of seasons
Keep breathing, keep inhaling
The air of life is good
And worth fighting for.

Derisha
Blocker

Don't stop

Keep going
Fatigue, stress
The things life throws at you
Is not at your best
The only way to make it
Is to keep going
Air in your lungs and rhythm of a heartbeat
Says keep going.

MOSS

Oh, the love a father can give
To his daughter and granddaughter
The love is unmatched to any
You made us laugh
Your laugh so contagious
It brought life to our entire being
You got on us when it was necessary
Sometimes your words didn't make us smile
But it was because you cared
You wanted us to be taken care of
You did your best to recover time
Time that was lost because life happened
I'm forever grateful to have had you in the time that I did
You are forever in my heart
I will forever be your princess
Growing into a queen
What you did for us was needed
No matter how great or small
It was appreciated and the memories will never be lost
I love you forever
And forever missing you.

Derisha
Blocker

I AM ME

Put on some shoes, matter fact
Walk in my shoes and then say my reaction is an attitude
Quiet and soft spoken
Turning the other cheek
Letting things roll off my shoulders
Cause I don't want no confrontation
Do you not know history?
From Harriet Tubman
Oprah Winfrey
Michelle Obama
And Maya Angelou
If that isn't enough roots run deep
I know who I am
By the looks of it you don't, and that's okay
The strength
The boldness
And the conviction in my voice
Might make you feel some-kind of way
But I am a true melanin woman
I've been up, I've down
But I still wear a crown
I speak up for myself
Stand up for myself
And I will
Don't speak
Until you've walked in my shoes.

All the Time

No one stays consistent in your corner all the time

It's important to choose wisely

And to discern always

When you get to that place of needing more

More support, more prayer

More encouraging

Remember that it all starts with yourself

Pray harder even with tears in your eyes

And when you want to give up

Holdfast to your faith

As hard as it gets people flake and walk away

Support yourself and encourage yourself

I know it feels better

When someone else lends a helping hand or word

But just know some are inconsistent

And would rather see you fall before you fly

You pick *you* every time

And you stay consistent in your own corner

All the time.

Derisha
Blocker

L.B.

Pain, I feel is untold
Pain, I don't want to feel
When I already live in a cold world
See
I was turkey
He was ham sandwich
I was one of the ones
I was the youngest girl
I was and will always be
DER-I-SHA

I was there when his bones became weak
I was there when he could barely speak
I was there when 9-1-1
Had to be dialed many times
God placed me there to help
To see
To witness
To be the voice
To bring a smile on his face
My heart misses him
My eyes miss seeing him
He fought a good fight
He overcame so much
Everything that should have taken him out
Did not
L.B. was strong
L.B. was bright
L.B. was tired
L.B. decided to take his rest
L.B., I love you, I will miss you forever.

Through
My Lens
Poetry

Good Place

How did I get in this place
This place of silence
The place where you can hear a leaf drop
Some would call it peace
Most would call it loneliness
I call it a season
The season to find who you are
To heal and regroup yourself
To recover from past hurts and shame
To see the bigger picture for your life
Seasons come and seasons go
When you enter one
Take advantage to learn
To learn the meaning of each season
Appearing to the eye, alone
You have company of yourself
Give your company love, joy, encouragement, forgiveness
And the assurance that this is only a season to grow
Grasp it, take hold of it
Make yourself better in this place.

Derisha
Blocker

Changing Me For <u>Me</u>

Oh, it doesn't feel good
To feel low, to feel anger
On the inside
Many have endured a lot of heartache and pain
But, have yet dug deep
To search and find the root of each feeling
Good or bad it's so vital to look within
To do some soul searching
To get down and dirty with your own self
Remove the blindfolds
Open deaf ears
To see you for who *you* really are
There's a deeper depth to go
To really get healed to really get free
I will be the first to tell you if no one else will
That this process of digging deep hurts
It's ugly, but so necessary
In the end of digging deep
Your soul will be happy
You will be new
Just because it doesn't feel good
Does not mean it's not good
Separating from toxic relationships and bad habits
Might cause a glitch in you
But once you are separated and start changing you
The road for you, gets much brighter.

Through
My Lens
Poetry

Not Alone

So many times, I said,
"I quit!"
"I give up."
"I am going to sit down."
"I throw in the towel!"
If you're like me you've been tried many times
Life has come and kept coming in full force
You might have felt isolated
You might have felt so alone
But when I tell you
God is on time, He is on time
Every time I gave up and sat myself down
God was right there nudging at me
He kept coming to see about me
He kept loving on me
He kept telling me,
"I am here."
"I will not leave you!"
He is a good - good Father
Just like He was and still is here for me
He is here for you
He loves you, He cares for you
You are a chosen vessel
And you will make it
So, get up, look up, and keep marching on
God got you
You are not alone.

Derisha
Blocker

Life Over Death

Anxiety kicks in
Hard to breathe
Shower water running
Couch is present
A seat is taken
Hard to catch my breath
I stare off in silence
Tears falling-down
I'm still sitting down in disbelief
Wondering what I'm going to do
Thinking
I'm not ready
What have I done
I'm not ready
This is not my other half
This is not it
Still tears hitting the ground
Hours have passed
Phone calls were made
A decision I had to make
Yes, choose life
No, choose death
There's purpose on the inside
Deep breaths taken
I finally said,
"Yes, to life."

Sonshine

Your face shining so bright like the sun
Your smile lights up the whole room
Your hugs are the greatest
Your kisses are the sweetest
You are one of the biggest blessings I've had thus far
To think, I was going to go the other way
Instead of having you
Is crazy
The truth is I wanted you
but fear paralyzed me
and caused me to consider something else
clear as day I heard God's voice,
"Keep him."
Strong as the wind I felt the presence of the Lord
And again, He pushed me to keep you
You're destined for greatness
You are a world changer
You are a champion
You are a miracle
You are my SONshine
And I'm glad to be chosen
As your mommy.

Derisha
Blocker

I Learned

I've learned to evaluate and reevaluate myself

This is a daily process

I find that I have a lot to fix and change within my own self

That I need healing and deliverance

From my past hurts and trauma

I notice that in the time I have alone

Is the time for this evaluation

To be transparent with myself

And to see myself with a corrective lens

There was a moment

Where true forgiveness took place during a situation

Where we both were able to say

Where we were wrong

We both demonstrated true love and forgiveness

Though it might have been difficult at first

We both realized that a misunderstanding

Was not worth a friendship

God spoke to her

And He spoke to me

What I loved the most that came from her lips was,

"You are not my enemy."

I continued to hear that

I began to think,
We war not against flesh and blood
But powers and principalities of this world
This self-evaluation phase of life
Is so important and it's very vital
To every one's growth

As I continue to work on the inward parts of myself, I want to encourage you to do the same. Do not let disagreements and misunderstandings cause hatred in your heart. Be quick to forgive and evaluate yourself in every situation. God wants us to demonstrate love and forgiveness towards each other quickly. Let's not allow bitterness and anger to control us any longer. Let's release it and love in Jesus's name.

> Scripture Reading: Ephesians 6:12
> For we do not wrestle against flesh and blood, but against principalities, against powers, against the rulers of the darkness of this age, against spiritual hosts of wickedness in the heavenly places.

Focused

Staying focus can be a super challenge
There's a lot in this world to distract us
From our goals, our passions, and our destiny
Be determined not to let anything stop you
And keep you down
I can honestly say that I have struggled
In this season with being focused
A lot of procrastination, social media time
And time where I thought I wasn't good enough
These skewed my focus
My eyes were taken off what I wanted
Instead, it was on something entirely different
But now, right now
I choose a focus mentality
They say press, so I'm pressing my way out
And into something greater
I'm focused now
With great focus comes great accomplishments.

Sigh

There are times when thoughts appear in the mind
Some positive some negative
It can get hard to fight those darts
Sent against the mind
Cast down one and realize that this fight
Is really the biggest battle in life
Continue declaring what the Bible says
And it then appears bigger and more frequent than before
Now you breakdown thinking you are all alone
With this battle
That very moment of *about to break*
He steps in only to say,

"Peace be still."
"I am with you."
"Here I am."
"I haven't left you."
"Rest in Me."
"Stop worrying and just believe I have it all under control."
"Walk in who I called you to be."
"Stop trying to figure out everything in between."
Again, Abba Father shows up
Like He does every time
So, Selah
Here comes the relief
Get up
And continue this journey of life.

Derisha
Blocker

Epilogue

You have reached the part of the poems that I call a pause. *Through My Lens,* a lot has happened. I've had many feelings of the good, the bad, and the ugly. Enough has happened to make me quit. Instead of quitting I continue to move forward. Moving forward when I am low is not always the easiest. There is always a push from God to keep going. The biggest push from Him is waking me up every day. I am reminded that with breath in my body and strength in my bones I am able to keep pressing forward.

This journey of life can be like a roller coaster, but I know my seatbelt is Jesus. He holds me together and loves me always, even when I'm at my worst. Knowing that my calling is bigger than me can get overwhelming, but I choose to trust and walk with Abba Father. When my vision gets blurry and my strength tends to fail, His hand holds me up and guides me where I need to be. I'm thankful that I am still here and it's only by God's grace and mercy. May He give you strength where you are weak and joy in place of sadness. May He grant you peace in chaos. I pray that you be blessed in your journey and that God keeps you always.

Final Message

We are healing every wound

Praying for mountains to be moved

Walking to the beat of our hearts'

Believing change is happening

Hoping for greater

Standing tall, even when we can't see

Waiting, though the waiting seems too hard to bear

For what we believe we will have

Let us not grow weary in well doing

Let us keep pressing towards the mark

Let us keep holding our heads' up

Knowing that greater is coming

Greater is our portion

Let's keep moving in upward motion

With purpose, with dignity

We will be the light for the world to see.

Derisha
Blocker

About the Author

Derisha Blocker is a woman of God who is dedicated to bringing positive change to young people and their situations. Moving towards her destiny, she hopes to fulfill everything God has set for her to do in the earth.

Derisha answered her call to minister in dance at the age of sixteen. Before her 'yes' to praise dancing, Derisha always loved dancing. Music was her outlet and brought life to her soul. To this very day she loves to dance and has a great time at every event she attends. After a couple of years of dancing for the Lord, by the age of eighteen, she became more committed and found that through praise dancing she was able to release everything life throws at her. Praise dancing is her outlet and her safe place and her first choice of worship.

Pursing her ministry in dance, led her to be the proud owner of Open Heaven Choreography LLC. The purpose of Open Heaven Choreography LLC is more than teaching dance to individuals and groups. It is to give hope where hope seems lost and to change the world through dance.

Derisha Blocker is on a journey to accomplish everything that has been delayed but certainly not denied. She currently has an Associate in Arts

Derisha
Blocker

General Education Degree. She is striving to finish school and continue to give her wonderful son an even better life.

With God, Derisha knows she will accomplish everything she puts her mind to. With Him, she knows that even bad days will not stop what God has destined to be for her present and future.

Open Heaven Choreography LLC
Email: ohdance21@gmail.com
Phone Number: 321-417-0553

www.ingramcontent.com/pod-product-compliance
Lightning Source LLC
Chambersburg PA
CBHW070940120626
46546CB00004B/1498